# best
## easy
# dayhikes

## Grand Teton

Bill Schneider

FALCON®

HELENA, MONTANA

# ＡFALCONGUIDE®

Falcon® Publishing is continually expanding its list of recreational guidebooks. All books include detailed descriptions, accurate maps, and all information necessary for enjoyable trips. You can order extra copies of this book and get information and prices for other Falcon® books by writing Falcon, P.O. Box 1718, Helena, MT 59624 or calling toll free 1-800-582-2665. Also, please ask for a free copy of our current catalog. Visit our website at www.FalconOutdoors.com, or contact us by e-mail at falcon@falcon.com.

© 1999 Falcon® Publishing, Inc., Helena, Montana.
Printed in Canada.

1 2 3 4 5 6 7 8 9 0 TP 03 02 01 00 99

Falcon and FalconGuide are registered trademarks of Falcon® Publishing, Inc.

Cataloging-in-Publication Data

Schneider, Bill.
    Best easy day hikes, Grand Teton / Bill Schneider.
        p. cm.—(Falcon guide)
    ISBN 1-56044-607-2 (pbk.)
    1. Hiking—Wyoming—Grand Teton National Park Guidebooks. 2. Grand Teton National Park (Wyo.) Guidebooks.    I. Title    II. Title: Grand Teton. III. Series.
GV199.42.W82G7366            1999
917.87'55—dc21                                              99-21225
                                                              CIP

## CAUTION

Outdoor recreational activities are by their very nature potentially hazardous. All participants in such activities must assume responsibility for their own actions and safety. The information contained in this guidebook cannot replace sound judgment and good decision-making skills, which help reduce risk exposure, nor does the scope of this book allow for disclosure of all the potential hazards and risks involved in such activities.

    Learn as much as possible about the outdoor recreational activities in which you participate, prepare for the unexpected, and be cautious. The reward will be a safer and more enjoyable experience.

# WILDERNESS is…

*The FREEDOM to experience true wildness…to hear only nature's music…to study the little secrets of the natural world…and to enjoy the quiet and solitude so rare in the stressful life we now live.*

*The CHALLENGE to learn and respect wild country…to be self-reliant…to take your time…to test your physical abilities…to courteously share the last blank spots on the map with others…and to fully enjoy your wilderness experience while leaving no trace of your passing.*

*The OPPORTUNITY to discover why wilderness is priceless…to see the threats to your wilderness…to decide to devote part of yourself to preserving it… and to encourage others to do the same.*

—Bill Schneider

# Grand Teton National Park

# Contents

# Introduction

## *What's a "best easy" day hike?*

It seems like there are two types of hikers—the more adventuresome types who like powerhiking or want to spend several days experiencing the depth of the wilderness and those who only have a day or two (or even just a few hours) and want a choice sample of the special features of a park or wilderness area. This book is for the second group.

There is a companion book, *Hiking Grand Teton National Park*, which includes long, strenuous day hikes and backpacking trips. This book is made up of the best and easiest hikes from this larger book.

*Hiking Grand Teton National Park* covers every trail in the park along with extensive related information to plan lengthy trips. This book includes only short, less strenuous day hikes that are my recommendations for the nicest day hikes in the park. The hikes vary in length and, with a few exceptions, have no big hills.

To make your choice as easy as possible, I have ranked the hikes from easiest to hardest, and they appear in the book in that manner. Christian Pond (the easiest) is listed first and Surprise and Amphitheater Lakes (the hardest) is listed last in the book.

Enjoy your best easy day hikes amid the incredible scenery of Grand Teton National Park.

1

# Ranking the Hikes

The following list ranks the hikes in this book from easiest to hardest.

**Easiest**    Christian Pond
Lakeshore Trail
String Lake
Swan Lake and Heron Pond
Moose Ponds
Lookout Rock
Willow Flats Shuttle
Leigh Lake
Grand View Point
Taggart Lake
Bradley Lake
Phelps Lake
Glade Creek
Willow Flats Loop
Two Ocean Lake
Jenny Lake
Cascade Canyon
Signal Mountain
Hermitage Point
**Hardest**    Surprise and Amphitheater Lakes

# Leave No Trace

Going into a national park such as Grand Teton National Park is like visiting a famous museum. You obviously do not want to leave your mark on an art treasure in the museum. If everybody going through the museum left one little mark, the piece of art would be quickly destroyed—and of what value is a big building full of trashed art? The same goes for a pristine wilderness such as Grand Teton, which is as magnificent as any masterpiece by any artist. If we all left just one little mark on the landscape, the wilderness would soon be despoiled.

A wilderness can accommodate human use as long as everybody behaves. But a few thoughtless or uninformed visitors can ruin it for everybody who follows. All wilderness users have a responsibility to know and follow the rules of no trace camping. An important source of these guidelines, including the most updated research, can be found in the book *Leave No Trace* (Falcon 1997). (Ordering information in the back of this book.)

Nowadays most wilderness users want to walk softly, but some aren't aware that they have poor manners. Often their actions are dictated by the outdated habits of a past generation of campers who cut green boughs for evening shelters, built campfires with fire rings, and dug trenches around tents. In the 1950s, these "camping rules" may have been acceptable, but they leave long-lasting scars, and today such behavior is absolutely unacceptable. The wilderness is shrinking, and the number of users is mushrooming. More and more camping areas show unsightly signs of heavy use.

Consequently, a new code of ethics is growing out of the necessity of coping with the unending waves of people who want a perfect wilderness experience. Today, we all must leave no clues that we have gone before. Canoeists can look behind the canoe and see no trace of their passing. Hikers, mountain bikers, and four-wheelers should have the same goal. Enjoy the wildness, but leave no trace of your visit.

---

## The Falcon Principles of Leave No Trace

- *Leave with everything you brought in.*
- *Leave no sign of your visit.*
- *Leave the landscape as you found it.*

---

Most of us know better than to litter—in or out of the wilderness. Be sure you leave nothing, regardless of how small it is, along the trail or at the campsite. This means you should pack out everything, including orange peels, flip tops, cigarette butts, and gum wrappers. Also, pick up any trash that others leave behind.

Follow the main trail. Avoid cutting switchbacks and walking on vegetation beside the trail.

Don't pick up "souvenirs," such as rocks, antlers, or wildflowers. The next person wants to see them, too, and collecting such souvenirs violates park regulations.

Avoid making loud noises that may disturb others. Remember, sound travels easily to the other side of the lake. Be courteous.

Carry a lightweight trowel to bury human waste 6–8 inches deep and pack out used toilet paper. Keep human waste at least 200 feet from any water source.

Finally, and perhaps most importantly, strictly follow the pack-in/pack-out rule. If you carry something into the backcountry, consume it or carry it out.

Leave no trace—and put your ear to the ground in the wilderness and listen carefully. Thousands of people coming behind you are thanking you for your courtesy and good sense.

# 1
# CHRISTIAN POND

**General description:** A short stroll from Jackson Lake Lodge for a good chance of seeing the rare trumpeter swan. Bring your binoculars.

**Type of trip:** Out and back.

**Total distance:** 1.2 miles.

**Starting point:** Jackson Lake Lodge Corral.

**Traffic:** Heavy, including heavy horse use.

**Maps:** Earthwalk Press Grand Teton Map, NPS handout map, and a Colter Bay Trail Guide brochure published by the Grand Teton Natural History Association.

**Finding the trailhead:** Take U.S. 89 15.2 miles south of the north boundary of the park and turn right (west) or go 1 mile north of the Jackson Lake Junction and turn left (west) into the Jackson Lake Lodge. Follow the signs and park in the corral parking lot.

**Parking and trailhead facilities:** There are restaurants, gift shops and restrooms in Jackson Lake Lodge. You can park either in the corral parking lot or in the main lot for the lodge.

**Key points:** None for this hike.

**The hike:** Christian Pond is a small lake mostly covered with pond lilies and other vegetation. It usually hosts nesting

# Christian Pond

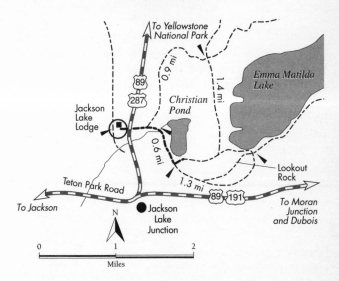

trumpeter swans that you can view from a safely distanced overlook.

To get there, take the very heavily used trail from the corral under the highway underpass. Large trail riding groups regularly leave from here, so plan on seeing lots of horses and being careful where you step.

The trail immediately goes under the highway underpass, and just past it you reach a trail junction. If you take the loop option, you return to this junction. Go right (east) here, and hike another 0.4 mile through open country to the Christian Pond Overlook. Spend some time here reading the interpretive signs and studying the swans and other

waterfowl commonly viewed on Christian Pond before re-
tracing your steps back to Jackson Lake Lodge.

**Options:** If 1.2 miles isn't enough hiking for you, this trip can
be extended to 3.1 miles. Continue past Christian Pond,
turn left (north) on the Grand View Point Trail and take
another left (west) 1.4 miles later. This takes you back to
the junction just east of the highway overpass.

# 2
# LAKESHORE TRAIL

**General description:** A short, flat walk along the scenic shore-line of Colter Bay and Jackson Lake.
**Type of trip:** Loop.
**Total distance:** 2 miles.
**Starting point:** Colter Bay Visitor Center.
**Traffic:** Heavy.
**Maps:** Earthwalk Press Grand Teton Map, NPS handout map, and a Colter Bay Trail Guide brochure published by the Grand Teton Natural History Association.

**Finding the trailhead:** Go 11 miles south of the park boundary on U.S. 89 or drive 5.2 miles north of the Jackson Lake Junction and turn west into the Colter Bay area. After turning off the main highway, go 0.7 mile to the visitor center, taking the first right turn after passing by the general store.

**Parking and trailhead facilities:** Park at the visitor center, which has restrooms. There is a general store a short walk east of the visitor center.

**Key points:**
0.3  End of paved road.
0.4  Dike at center of "figure 8" route.
1.5  Cross dike again.
1.9  Amphitheater.
2.0  Visitor center.

# Lakeshore Trail

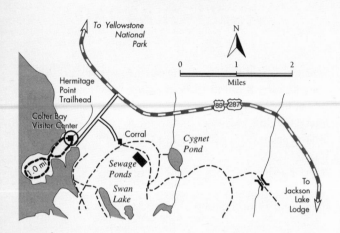

**The hike:** This hike is a great choice for an evening or early morning stroll, especially for campers staying in the Colter Bay area or for families with kids. The kids can help fill up Jackson Lake by throwing countless stones into it.

The "trail" actually starts out as a paved service road (no vehicles allowed) through the boat dock area and then turns into a well-used, single-track trail. About one-tenth of a mile after the road ends, you reach a trail sign and then a dike across a narrow section of land out into a small island. The dike forms the center of this "figure 8" route.

The trail circles the island (actually a small peninsula in Colter Bay), staying close to the water most of the way. Several beach areas invite you to stop and soak in the scenery of the Teton Range, especially Mount Moran, across the vast surface of Jackson Lake.

When you reach the bridge again, turn left and finish the "figure 8" route. You come out by an NPS amphitheater where rangers give talks. Check at the visitor center for a schedule.

**Options:** The "figure 8" loop can be done in either direction with no increase in difficulty.

# 3
# STRING LAKE

**General description:** A short hike around a small placid lake.
**Type of trip:** Loop.
**Total distance:** 3.4 miles.
**Starting point:** String Lake Trailhead.
**Traffic:** Moderate on west side, heavy on east side.
**Maps:** Earthwalk Press Grand Teton Map and NPS hand-out map.

**Finding the trailhead:** Take U.S. 89 north of Jackson for 11.5 miles and turn left (west) at the Moose Junction. Drive past the Moose Visitor Center and through the entrance station (1 mile after turning off highway). Follow this paved park road for another 9.7 miles from the entrance station to the Jenny Lake turnoff. Turn left (west) here and drive 0.6 mile (follow the signs and take two right turns) to the String Lake Trailhead and 0.3 mile farther, the String Lake Picnic Area. The Leigh Lake Trailhead is in the northwest corner of the picnic area. If you're coming from the north, drive 9.9 miles from the Jackson Lake Junction and turn right (west) at the Jenny Lake turnoff.

**Parking and trailhead facilities:** Park in large parking lots at the String Lake Trailhead. There are no toilet facilities right at the String Lake Trailhead, but you can find them at the nearby picnic area.

# String Lake

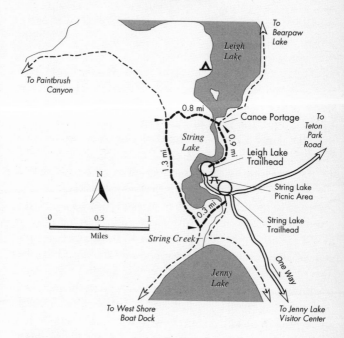

## Key points:
0.3  String Lake Picnic Area.
0.7  Horse trail comes in from east.
1.1  End of String Lake and junction with loop trail.
1.2  Bridge over String Creek.
1.8  Junction with Paintbrush Canyon Trail.
3.1  Junction with Jenny Lake Trail.
3.3  Bridge over String Creek.
3.4  String Lake Trailhead.

**The hike:** Short hikes really don't get much nicer than this one, a flat loop around a gorgeous mountain lake in the shadow of the high peaks. It's also a good choice for an early season hike because the snow usually leaves the area long before it gives up the high country.

The first 0.3 mile of the String Lake Trail is wheelchair accessible, with cathedralistic views of the Teton Range over placid String Lake. This is a "piedmont lake" formed by valley glaciers at the head of Paintbrush Canyon. The same goes for Jenny Lake at the head of Cascade Canyon and Leigh Lake at the head of Leigh Canyon.

After passing by the picnic area and related parking lot, the trail is no longer wheelchair accessible, but is still double wide and in terrific shape with more sandy beaches and outstanding views.

At the end of the lake, go left (west) at the junction. You immediately reach a long footbridge over the short but scenic stream connecting String Lake and Leigh Lake. From the bridge, walk through a mature forest up to the junction with the Paintbrush Canyon Trail. Go left (south) here, and walk through mostly open terrain down to the west shoreline of String Lake. The views are not quite as nice here with no Teton Range backdrop, but they are still well worth it. At the next junction, go left (east), cross the unnamed stream between String Lake and Jenny Lake on another big footbridge, and you're back at the trailhead.

**Options:** This loop hike can be taken in either direction with no extra difficulty.

**Side trips:** If you need more hiking, you can hike down to the head of Jenny Lake (0.4 mile round trip) or the foot of Leigh Lake (0.3 mile round trip).

# 4
# SWAN LAKE AND
# HERON POND

**General description:** An easy circuit with special treats for wild-life watchers.
**Type of trip:** A "lollipop" loop.
**Total distance:** 3 miles.
**Starting point:** Hermitage Point Trailhead.
**Traffic:** Heavy.
**Maps:** Earthwalk Press Grand Teton Map, NPS handout map, and a Colter Bay Trail Guide brochure published by the Grand Teton Natural History Association.

**Finding the trailhead:** Take U.S. 89 into the park and turn west into the Colter Bay area, which is 11 miles south of the park's northern boundary or 5.2 miles north of the Jackson Lake Junction. The trailhead is a little hard to find the first time you go into the Colter Bay area. It's located at the south end of the big parking lot near the boat launch. After turning into Colter Bay from the main highway, drive 0.9 mile on a paved road to the trailhead, then turn left (south) at the first turn after passing the general store. Be careful not to take the trail that heads off to the east behind the trailhead sign. Instead, walk to the end of the parking lot toward the boat launch where there are trailhead signs marking the beginning of the trail.

# Swan Lake and Heron Pond

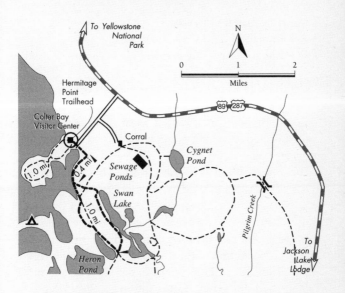

**Parking and trailhead facilities:** Park in the large parking lot at the trailhead. The lot is also used by people launching boats. Go to the visitor center (just north of trailhead) for toilet facilities. You pass a general store on the way to the trailhead.

## Key points:

0.4  Junction with Swan Lake Trail.
0.6  Junction with Jackson Lake Overlook Trail, alternate route.
0.9  Jackson Lake Overlook Trail rejoins main trail.
1.0  Heron Pond.

1.4 Four-way junction.
2.1 Swan Lake.
2.5 Junction with trail to corral.
2.6 Rejoin main trail to Colter Bay area.
3.0 Hermitage Point Trailhead.

**The hike:** Be sure to take a map and plan on closely noting the directional signs along the route. There are several junctions along this short loop, and if you're enjoying the scenery too thoroughly (which would be easy), you might get on the wrong trail.

The trail starts out as a service road (it has a locked gate and is only occasionally used by vehicles). Along this stretch of trail you can enjoy outstanding views of Colter Bay, with Mount Moran providing a classic backdrop.

At the end of the dirt road, you reach the first junction where the loop section of this trip begins. Go right (south), unless you decide to take the route in reverse. The trail turns into well-used singletrack, but is still in excellent shape.

About two-tenths of a mile later, you reach a fork in the trail. If you don't mind a little hill, go right for a nice view from the Jackson Lake Overlook. Either trail takes you to Heron Pond about one-half mile later.

Heron Pond is mostly covered with pond lilies. You can usually see pelicans, Canada geese, and other waterfowl species on the pond. In the evening hours, you might see beavers dining on the pond lilies, and you might see a moose in the willows that surround the pond.

At the south end of Heron Pond, you reach a four-way trail junction. Take the sharpest left turn and head up a small hill toward Swan Lake.

Like Heron Pond, Swan Lake is covered with yellow pond lilies. The lake gets its name from the two trumpeter swans that have lived here since the 1980s. The rare swans have never produced any young, but they have fiercely defended their territory, chasing away other swans that might have successfully nested in this prime habitat.

After the lake, you pass by abandoned sewage ponds and then come to a junction with a trail heading off to the right (north) to the Colter Bay Corral. Go left (west) and 0.1 mile later, rejoin the abandoned service road for a 0.4-mile walk back to the trailhead.

**Options:** This loop can be taken in reverse with no increase in difficulty.

**Side trips:** If you want a longer hike, you can add to your day by hiking down to Hermitage Point.

# 5
# MOOSE PONDS

**General description:** A short loop hike for wildlife watchers.
**Type of trip:** Loop.
**Total distance:** 2.6 miles.
**Starting point:** South Jenny Visitor Center.
**Traffic:** Moderate.
**Maps:** Earthwalk Press Grand Teton Map and NPS handout map.

**Finding the trailhead:** Take U.S. 89 north of Jackson for 11.5 miles and turn left (west) at the Moose Junction. Drive past the Moose Visitor Center and through the entrance station (1 mile after turning off highway). Follow this paved park road for another 6.8 miles from the entrance station to the South Jenny Lake turnoff. Turn left (west) here and drive less than one-half mile to the visitor center. If you're coming from the north, drive 12.8 miles from the Jackson Lake Junction and turn right (west) at the South Jenny Lake turnoff.

**Parking and trailhead facilities:** The South Jenny Lake area has a general store, visitor center, boat dock, toilet facilities, and usually plenty of room to park. This is a heavily used area, and the boat ride across the lake is very popular, so in midday during the summer, the parking lot is often full.

# Moose Ponds

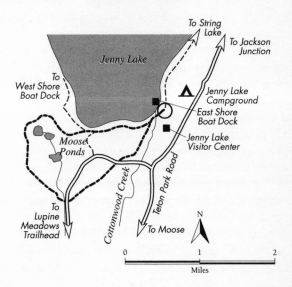

**Key points:**

0.1 Footbridge over Cottonwood Creek, the outlet to Jenny Lake.

0.3 Boat launching area.

0.6 Junction with Moose Ponds Trail.

2.0 Lupine Meadows Road.

2.3 Lupine Meadows Road.

2.5 Exum Climbing School.

2.6 South Jenny Lake Visitor Center.

**The hike:** The area around South Jenny Lake is heavily developed—and a bit confusing to the first-time visitor. Fortunately, if necessary, you can get your questions answered in the visitor center.

From the visitor center, start following the trail around the south edge of the lake. You immediately cross over Cottonwood Creek (outlet to Jenny Lake), along the north edge of a road, and pass the boat-launching area before getting to what looks like a real trail.

Follow this trail for less than one-half mile to the junction with Moose Ponds Trail, which is on top of a glacial moraine at the south end of Jenny Lake. Go left (west) here, and drop down a short but steep slope to the Moose Ponds. The trail winds through willow flats and over footbridges around the three ponds. Watch for elk and moose on the slopes above and waterfowl on the ponds.

After leaving the Moose Ponds, go through a short section of mature forest and then out into the sagebrush flats of Lupine Meadows. The last mile of the hike can also be confusing as you cross the unpaved road to Lupine Meadows Trailhead twice and go behind the Exum Climbing School before getting back to the South Jenny Lake area.

**Options:** This loop hike can be taken in either direction with no extra difficulty. You can also make this an add-on to the Jenny Lake hike.

# 6
# LOOKOUT ROCK

**General description:** An ideal small loop hike from Jackson Lake Lodge.
**Type of trip:** A "lollipop" loop.
**Total distance:** 3.8 miles.
**Starting point:** Jackson Lake Lodge Corral.
**Traffic:** Heavy, including heavy horse use.
**Maps:** Earthwalk Press Grand Teton Map, NPS handout map, and a Colter Bay Trail Guide brochure published by the Grand Teton Natural History Association.

**Finding the trailhead:** Take U.S. 89 15.2 miles south of the north boundary of the park or 1 mile north of the Jackson Lake Junction and turn west into the Jackson Lake Lodge. Follow the signs and park at the corral parking lot.

**Parking and trailhead facilities:** There are restaurants, gift shops and restrooms in the lodge. Park at the corral parking lot or the main lot at the lodge.

## Key points:
0.2  Junction just past highway underpass.
0.6  Christian Pond Overlook and junction.
1.5  Junction with Lookout Rock Cutoff Trail.
2.3  Junction with south shore trail.
2.4  Lookout Rock and junction with cutoff trail.

# Lookout Rock

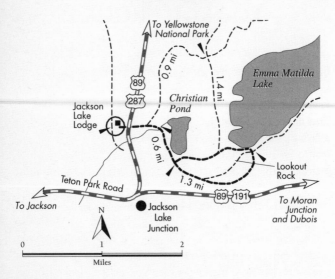

2.6 Junction with Grand View Point Trail.
3.2 Christian Pond Overlook.
3.6 Junction with trail before underpass.
3.8 Jackson Lake Lodge Corral.

**The hike:** If you're looking for a short walk after dinner or early morning during your stay at Jackson Lake Lodge, you couldn't do much better than this hike. You get a chance to see rare trumpeter swans nesting on Christian Pond, study the great Oxbow Bend of the Snake River, and enjoy a view of massive Emma Matilda Lake from Lookout Rock.

From the corral, take the very heavily used trail from the corral and under the highway underpass. Large trail riding groups regularly leave from here, so plan on seeing lots of horses and being careful where you step.

Just past the underpass, go right (southeast) at a junction and hike another 0.4 mile through open country to the Christian Pond Overlook. Spend some time here reading the interpretive signs and studying the swans and other waterfowl commonly viewed on Christian Pond, then take the trail to the right (southeast) toward the Oxbow Bend of the Snake River.

This trail goes through the open sagebrush- and balsamroot-covered slope above U.S. 287 and the Oxbow Bend of the Snake River. Take a few moments along the way to see how the Snake River has severely meandered and then cut through to create a small oxbow lake. You can often see pelicans and swans floating on the lake even from a great distance. You also get a good view of Jackson Lake and Donaho Point Island, with the Teton Range as a dramatic backdrop.

After 0.9 mile you reach a junction with a cutoff trail to Lookout Rock. You can turn left here and cut about one-quarter mile off the trip, but I recommend continuing on the Oxbow Bend Trail. It's more scenic with less horse use. These two trails join the trail along the south shoreline of Emma Matilda Lake on each side of Lookout Rock.

Enjoy a rest and the vista from Lookout Rock Overlook before heading back toward Christian Pond. When you get to the Grand View Point Trail junction, go left (west) and go another 0.6 mile back to Christian Pond. From here retrace your steps back to Jackson Lake Lodge.

**Options:** You can knock about one-quarter mile off the hike by taking the Lookout Rock Cutoff Trail. You can also do this loop in reverse with no increased difficulty.

# 7
# WILLOW FLATS SHUTTLE

**General description:** An easy walk through wildlife-rich flatland.
**Type of trip:** Shuttle.
**Total distance:** 4.9 miles.
**Starting point:** Jackson Lake Lodge.
**Traffic:** Heavy, including heavy horse use.
**Maps:** Earthwalk Press Grand Teton Map, NPS handout map, and a Colter Bay Trail Guide brochure published by the Grand Teton Natural History Association.

**Finding the trailhead:** Drive 15.2 miles south on U.S. 89 south of the park boundary or 1 mile north of the Jackson Lake Junction with U.S. 287 and turn west into the well-marked Jackson Lake Lodge area. The trail actually starts in a small parking area on the south side of the main lodge. Leave a vehicle or arrange to be picked up at the Colter Bay Corral. Colter Bay is 4.2 miles northwest of Jackson Lake Lodge on U.S. 89. After turning west into the Colter Bay area, follow the signs and park in the corral parking lot.

**Parking and trailhead facilities:** Park in the Jackson Lake Lodge parking lot to use the restrooms or enjoy the restaurants and gift shops in the lodge.

# Willow Flats Shuttle

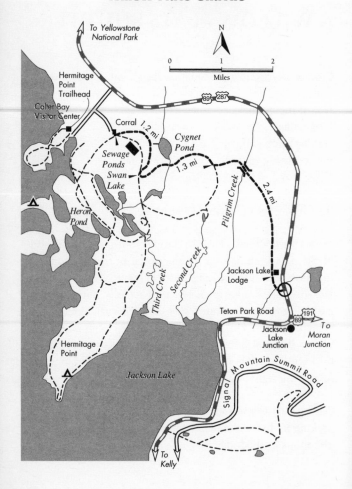

**Key points:**
2.4 Junction with trail down Second Creek.
3.7 Junction with trail to Hermitage Point.
4.9 Colter Bay Corral.

**The hike:** This is a great hike for people staying at Jackson Lake Lodge or Colter Bay, but pick a cool day because the route goes through open meadows and willow flats with little shade along the way. Unlike trails in the high canyons of the Teton Range, snow leaves this area earlier in the spring and usually doesn't come as soon in the fall, which makes this route ideal for spring or fall hiking.

As far as shuttle hikes go, this is one of the easiest. It's only a short drive from Jackson Lake Lodge to leave your vehicle at Colter Bay Corral. You can also leave the vehicle in the Colter Bay parking area, but that is about 0.4 mile farther.

The route starts right behind Jackson Lake Lodge on a mostly abandoned jeep road, which is closed to the public but used occasionally by concessionaires serving meals to horse riding groups. Actually, the entire route is on a dirt road, but it's still a pleasant hike, especially for hikers who get nervous about being too far from civilization and like perfectly flat hikes.

The first mile or so of the road goes through a large freshwater marsh. This is a wildlife-rich area, so you stand a good chance of seeing coyotes, moose, sandhill cranes, and other large wildlife species, as well as a wealth of smaller birds. You go by two classic beaver ponds and over Spring

Creek on a bridge. You also get a great view of the Teton Range across Jackson Lake along the first part of the hike.

After crossing the freshwater marsh, cross over Pilgrim Creek on a massive concrete bridge. Long ago, this was the main route into Jackson Hole. After U.S. 89 was constructed, this became a hiking trail with a monstrous, out-of-character bridge.

As you near the first junction, you enter a mixed forest area dominated by a stand of stately cottonwoods. When you reach the junction, take a right (northwest) and head toward Colter Bay. As you approach this junction, watch for a single-track trail angling off to the right and cutting 200 yards off the trip when it rejoins the road.

After the junction, the cottonwoods gradually give way to conifers. At the second junction, go right (north) and return to the corral.

**Options:** This can be turned into a delightful "lollipop" loop hike. Refer to the Willow Flats Loop hike description. You can also start at Colter Bay instead of Jackson Lake Lodge with no increase in difficulty.

# 8
# LEIGH LAKE

**General description:** A short, flat hike along the shoreline of two lakes.

**Type of trip:** Out and back.

**Total distance:** 5.4 miles.

**Starting point:** Leigh Lake Trailhead at the String Lake Picnic Area.

**Traffic:** Heavy, including heavy horse traffic.

**Maps:** Earthwalk Press Grand Teton Map and NPS handout map.

**Finding the trailhead:** Take U.S. 89 north of Jackson for 11.5 miles and turn left (west) at the Moose Junction. Drive past the Moose Visitor Center and through the entrance station (1 mile after turning off the highway). Follow this paved park road for another 9.7 miles from the entrance station to the Jenny Lake turnoff. Turn left (west) here and drive 0.6 mile (follow the signs and take two right turns) to the String Lake Trailhead and 0.3 mile farther, the String Lake Picnic Area. The Leigh Lake Trailhead is in the northwest corner of the picnic area. If you're coming from the north, drive 9.9 miles from the Jackson Lake Junction and turn right (west) at the Jenny Lake turnoff.

**Parking and trailhead facilities:** Park in the large parking lot at the picnic area. There are toilet facilities in the picnic area at the Leigh Lake Trailhead.

# Leigh Lake

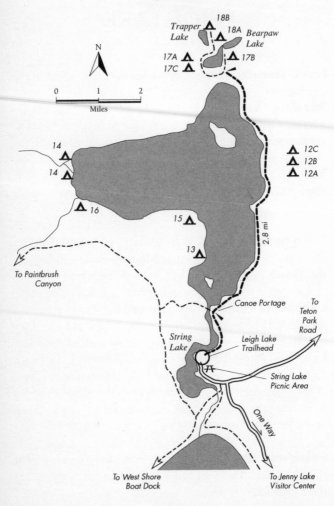

**Key points:**
0.4 Horse trail comes in from east.
0.8 End of String Lake and junction with Holly Lake Trail.
1.0 Leigh Lake.
2.4 East Shore camps.
2.8 End of Leigh Lake.

**The hike:** Although Leigh Lake is also a nice hike in July, August, and September, it's a great choice in May or June. The snow leaves this area much sooner than the high country. The scenery is unbeatable with Mount Moran and Rockchuck Peak looming above Leigh Lake and narrow Paintbrush and Leigh Canyons slicing into the Teton Range above the west shore on each side of Mount Woodring, the high peak between Mount Moran and Rockchuck Peak.

The trail is in terrific shape (often double wide) all the way, and sandy beaches provide inviting rest spots along both String Lake and Leigh Lake.

Halfway along String Lake, there is a horse trail coming in from the right (east). From this point on, don't be surprised to see a string of horses with park visitors getting their first horse-riding experience. At the end of String Lake, go right (north) at the junction. At this point, you see a portage trail for people hauling their canoes up to Leigh Lake. The foot trail angles off to the right of the portage trail.

After a short, 0.2-mile walk through lodgepole pines, you get your first view of enormous Leigh Lake, a 250-foot-deep lake formed by the glaciers that once flowed out of

Leigh and Paintbrush Canyons. The trail goes along the shoreline with Mount Moran providing the scenic backdrop.

About halfway along Leigh Lake, you pass by the East Shore campsites complete with sandy beaches and world-record vistas. The end of the lake is about three-tenths of a mile past the campsites. You can turn around at the campsites or the end of the lake.

**Options:** If you don't want to retrace your steps all the way back, you can turn right (west) at the junction at the end of String Lake and take the String Lake loop trail back to the picnic area. This adds 2.5 miles to your hike.

**Side trips:** If you need more hiking, you can hike up to Bearpaw Lake, which adds 2.4 miles to the total distance. Or you can add another 0.8 mile by going up to Trapper Lake.

# 9
# GRAND VIEW POINT

**General description:** A short, steep hike with a view to dream for.

**Type of trip:** Out and back with loop option.

**Total distance:** 2.2 miles.

**Starting point:** Grand View Point Trailhead.

**Traffic:** Moderate.

**Maps:** Earthwalk Press Grand Teton Map, NPS handout map, and a Colter Bay Trail Guide brochure published by the Grand Teton Natural History Association.

**Finding the trailhead:** Drive 0.9 mile north of the Jackson Lake Lodge turnoff on U.S. 89 and turn right (east) on an unpaved road. When I hiked this trip, this turnoff was unmarked, but it's the first right turn north of Jackson Lake Lodge. This is a rough jeep road for high-clearance vehicles only. Drive 0.8 mile up this jeep road until it ends at the trailhead.

**Parking and trailhead facilities:** If you have a high-clearance vehicle, park right at the trailhead. If not, park in one of the turnouts along the first part of the jeep road and walk up the road to the trailhead. There are no trailhead facilities.

**The hike:** This is a wonderful short hike, but you have a serious hill to climb to earn the spectacular view from Grand View Point.

# Grand View Point

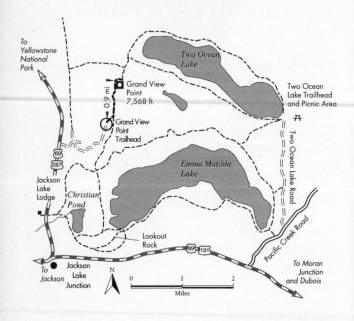

Just uphill from the trailhead (0.2 mile), you come to a junction with a trail heading south toward Emma Matilda Lake. Go left (north) here, and start a gradual climb up to the top of Grand View Point. Just before you reach Grand View Point, you level off at a high point that could be confused with the real thing. Walk slightly farther down the trail for the real Grand View Point.

From the top of 7,586-foot Grand View Point, you get the view you expected, an outstanding look at Mount Moran and the rest of the mighty Teton Range off to the west, although this is partially obscured by trees. However, to my surprise, you also get a terrific, sweeping vista of Two Ocean Lake, the lush meadows surrounding this huge mountain lake, and the Teton Wilderness in the background.

After a short rest, enjoy the downhill walk back to the trailhead.

**Options:** You can make a short loop out of this trip by continuing on the trail down the north side of Grand View Point for 0.9 mile to a junction with the Pilgrim Creek Trail. Go left (west) here and hike 1 mile until you get into a large meadow. Here, the trail turns into an abandoned jeep road. Walk down the jeep road a few hundred yards until you see another road heading off to the south. Go left here and in 0.8 mile you join the jeep road you drove up to the trailhead. Turn left (east) here and walk up the road to your vehicle. Total distance of loop—4.4 miles.

**Side trips:** You could hike down to the west end of Two Ocean Lake (2.6 miles round trip from Grand View Point) before heading back to the trailhead.

# 10
# TAGGART LAKE

**General description:** A short hike to a low-elevation lake.
**Type of trip:** Loop.
**Total distance:** 4 miles.
**Starting point:** Taggart Lake Trailhead.
**Traffic:** Heavy.
**Maps:** Earthwalk Press Grand Teton Map and NPS trail guide to Taggart and Bradley Lakes.

**Finding the trailhead:** Take U.S. 89 north of Jackson for 11.5 miles and turn left (west) at the Moose Junction. Drive past the Moose Visitor Center and through the entrance station (1 mile after turning off highway). Follow this paved park road for another 2.2 miles from the entrance station and turn left (west) into the Taggart Lake Trailhead. If you're coming from the north, drive 17.4 miles from the Jackson Lake Junction and turn right (west) into the trailhead parking lot.

**Parking and trailhead facilities:** This trailhead has toilet facilities and plenty of parking.

# Taggart Lake

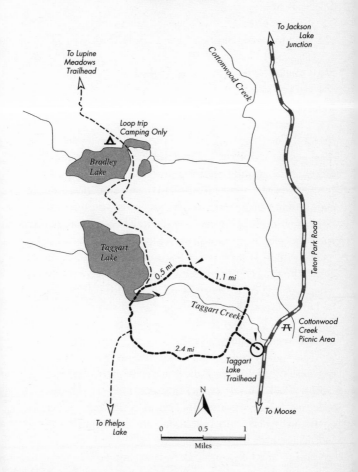

To Jackson Lake Junction

Cottonwood Creek

To Lupine Meadows Trailhead

Loop trip Camping Only

Bradley Lake

Taggart Lake

0.5 mi

1.1 mi

Teton Park Road

Taggart Creek

Cottonwood Creek Picnic Area

2.4 mi

Taggart Lake Trailhead

To Phelps Lake

To Moose

N

0        0.5        1
Miles

**Key points:**

0.3  Start of loop trail.
0.8  Taggart Creek.
1.0  Junction with Bradley Lake Cutoff Trail.
1.6  Taggart Lake.
2.4  Junction with Beaver Creek Trail.
3.8  End of loop.
4.0  Taggart Lake Trailhead.

**The hike:** The short loop hike to Taggart Lake, named for the chief geologist of the 1872 Hayden Expedition, is one of the most accessible and popular short day hikes in the park.

The first 0.2 mile of the trail to the first junction is double wide and flat and goes through a sagebrush-dotted meadow. Here, go right (northwest) and the trail becomes singletrack and goes past some minor development and over Taggart Creek, which you cross on a sturdy footbridge. After the creek, the trail climbs gradually up to the top of a moraine where you get consistently good views of the Teton Range, including Grand Teton. This section of the trail also goes through an old forest fire burn, so you can observe how the forest is regenerating.

The trail is in great shape all the way with a few rocky sections. When you reach the junction with the Bradley Lake Cutoff Trail, go left (west) and continue for another 0.6 mile to the lake and the junction with the Valley Trail. Go left (south) here, and hike along the lakeshore to a large footbridge over the outlet.

Forest-lined Taggart Lake sits at only 6,902 feet at the foot of Avalanche Canyon. You get a gorgeous view of the

Grand Teton over the lake on the horizon. You can look around and see how glaciers left a moraine, which formed a natural dam to create the lake.

After leaving the lake, you hike on the Valley Trail for 0.8 mile to the junction with the Beaver Creek Trail. Go left (east) and follow Beaver Creek until you climb over a small hill (bigger if you take the loop counterclockwise) and drop down to the sagebrush flat to the junction with the loop trail and back to the trailhead.

**Options:** You can take the loop in either direction with no increase in difficulty.

# Bradley Lake

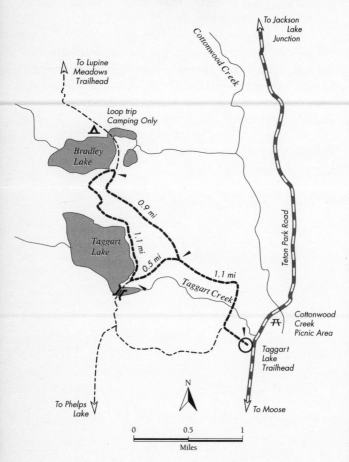

# 11
# BRADLEY LAKE

**General description:** A short hike to a low-elevation lake.
**Type of trip:** A "lollipop" loop.
**Total distance:** 5.3 miles.
**Starting point:** Taggart Lake Trailhead.
**Traffic:** Moderate.
**Maps:** Earthwalk Press Grand Teton Map and NPS trail guide to Taggart and Bradley Lakes.

**Finding the trailhead:** Take U.S. 89 north of Jackson for 11.5 miles and turn left (west) at the Moose Junction. Drive past the Moose Visitor Center and through the entrance station (1 mile after turning off the highway). Follow this paved park road for another 2.2 miles from the entrance station and turn left (west) into the Taggart Lake Trailhead. If you're coming from the north, drive 17.4 miles from the Jackson Lake Junction and turn right (west) into the trailhead parking lot.

**Parking and trailhead facilities:** This trailhead has toilet facilities and plenty of parking.

**Key points:**
0.2  Start of loop trail.
0.7  Taggart Creek.
1.3  Junction with Bradley Lake Cutoff Trail.

2.2  Bradley Lake and junction with Valley Trail.
3.3  Taggart Lake and junction with Taggart Lake Trail.
4.0  Junction with Bradley Lake Cutoff Trail.
5.1  Junction with loop trail.
5.3  Taggart Lake Trailhead.

**The hike:** Bradley Lake, like Taggart Lake, was named for a member of the 1872 Hayden expedition and, also like Taggart Lake, is one of the most accessible and popular short day hikes in the park.

The first 0.2 mile of the trail to the first junction is double wide and flat and goes through a sagebrush-dotted meadow. Here, go right (northwest) and the trail becomes singletrack and goes past some minor development and on to Taggart Creek, which you cross on a sturdy footbridge. After the creek, the trail climbs gradually up to the top of a moraine where you get consistently good views of the Teton Range, including Grand Teton. This section of the trail also goes through a 1996 forest fire burn, so you can observe how the forest regenerates itself.

You see the Bradley Lake Cutoff Trail 1.3 miles from the trailhead. Turn right (north) here and continue through another mile of the same terrain to 7,022-foot Bradley Lake, a deep pool at the foot of Garnet Canyon, impounded there long ago when the glacier flowing out of the canyon melted.

At this point you can retrace your steps to the trailhead, but it only adds 0.7 mile to make a loop and see two lakes instead of one. If you prefer the loop option, take a left (south) on the Valley Trail connecting Bradley and Taggart Lakes and climb over a short but steep ridge (actually another moraine) between the lakes.

It's only 1.1 miles to forest-lined Taggart Lake, which is at a slightly lower elevation (6,902 feet) but otherwise similar to Bradley Lake. I liked the view from Taggart better than from Bradley, but they are both beautiful mountain lakes.

Before you reach the footbridge over the outlet of Taggart Lake, turn left (east) on the Taggart Lake Trail and follow it for 0.5 mile back to the junction with the Bradley Lake Cutoff Trail. From here, retrace your steps back to the trailhead.

**Options:** You can take the loop in either direction with no increase in difficulty. You can also take the out-and-back option, or you can add another 0.8 mile to the hike by following the Valley Trail south past Taggart Lake to the junction with the Beaver Creek Trail. Turn left (east) here and follow the trail back to the Taggart Lake Trailhead. This option makes a true loop out of this trip.

# Phelps Lake

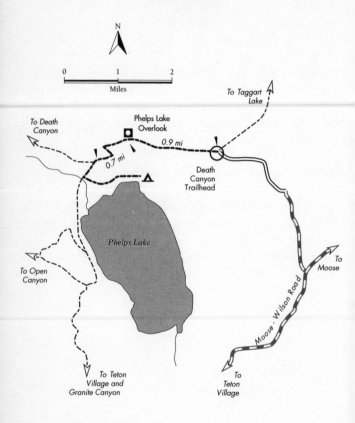

# 12
# PHELPS LAKE

**General description:** A short hike to a low-elevation lake.
**Type of trip:** Out and back.
**Total distance:** 4 miles.
**Starting point:** Whitegrass/Death Canyon Trailhead.
**Traffic:** Heavy.
**Maps:** Earthwalk Press Grand Teton Map and NPS hand-out map.

**Finding the trailhead:** The trailhead is called Whitegrass on some maps and signs and Death Canyon on others, but it's the same place.

From Jackson, take Wyoming Highway 22 west for 6 miles to the Moose-Wilson Road Junction just before entering the small town of Wilson. Turn right (north) here, go past Teton Village into the park, and continue on this road (which turns to gravel) until you see the Death Canyon Trailhead turnoff on your left (west), 11.5 miles from Wyoming Highway 22. If you're coming from the north, the trailhead is 3.1 miles south of the Moose Visitor Center on the Moose-Wilson Road, which turns south right across from the visitor center and doesn't go through the entrance station.

After turning off the Moose-Wilson Road, drive 1.6 miles to the actual trailhead, the last mile of which is an unpaved road that can get rough. The NPS recommends a high-clearance vehicle for this road.

**Parking and trailhead facilities:** The trailhead has toilet facilities and a fairly large parking area, but this trailhead is so popular that it can be full, especially at midday.

**Key points:**
0.1 Junction with Valley Trail.
0.9 Phelps Lake Overlook.
1.6 Junction with Death Canyon Trail.
2.0 Phelps Lake.

**The hike:** Phelps Lake is one of the most popular destinations in the park. It is on the Valley Trail, which goes from Teton Village to the Lupine Meadows Trailhead. You can reach it from several trailheads, but the shortest, most popular route starts at the Death Canyon Trailhead (also called Whitegrass Trailhead on some maps and signs).

Only 0.1 mile after leaving the trailhead parking lot, you reach the first junction with the Valley Trail. Go left (southwest) here, and hike 0.8 mile up a gradual hill to the Phelps Lake Overlook, where you get a nice view of the lake and the valley beyond.

From here, it's a steep downhill on switchbacks to the lake with a left (south) turn at the junction with the trail up Death Canyon. If you're camping, take a left on a spur trail just as you get to the lake instead of following the Valley Trail along the west side of the lake.

The well-maintained trail goes through mature forest most of the way with one brush-covered open slope above Phelps Lake. Watch for moose and black bears, which are commonly seen around Phelps Lake. Enjoy some fishing (with a Wyoming state fishing license) for brook, cutthroat, and lake trout. After your stay at Phelps Lake, retrace your steps back to the trailhead, keeping in mind that the way back involves a fairly steep climb up to the Phelps Lake Overlook.

**Options:** You can make this a shuttle by leaving a vehicle at the Granite Canyon Trailhead, which would make this a 6.1-mile hike.

# 13
# GLADE CREEK

**General description:** A short, easy hike in the northernmost section of the park.
**Type of trip:** Out and back.
**Total distance:** 7 miles.
**Starting point:** Glade Creek Trailhead.
**Traffic:** Light.
**Maps:** Earthwalk Press Grand Teton Map and NPS handout map.

**Finding the trailhead:** From U.S. 89, drive 4.4 miles west of Flagg Ranch on the Grassy Lake Road (also known as Ashton-Flagg Ranch Road) and park at the trailhead on the left (south) side of the road.

**Parking and trailhead facilities:** Park in the small lot at the trailhead, which has a pit toilet.

**Key points:**
1.5  Cross the Glade Creek footbridge.
2.0  Break out into a big meadow.
3.5  Park boundary.

**The hike:** Most people don't think about this section of Grand Teton National Park, so plan on having Glade Creek and most of the north trails section mostly to yourself. This hike

# Glade Creek

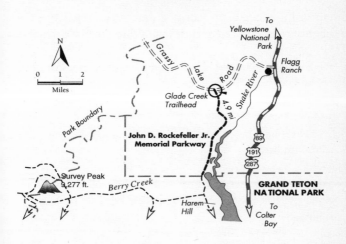

actually starts outside of the park in the John D. Rockefeller Jr. Memorial Parkway, but the area is just as undeveloped as the park itself—in fact, it is more wild than many parts of the park. The trailhead sign says that it's 3.5 miles to the park boundary, but this is probably exaggerated by at least one-half mile and perhaps more.

The trail starts out through a mature lodgepole forest. You cross Glade Creek on a footbridge at about the 1.5-mile mark. Shortly thereafter, you drop down a fairly steep hill to a massive meadow. To the left, you can see the Snake River flowing into Jackson Lake and a huge freshwater marsh, the second large freshwater marsh found in the park. (The other is just south and west of the Jackson Lake Lodge.)

You can also see Jackson Lake off to the south, and you may also be able to see some moose, swans, and other wildlife, especially in the early morning or near sunset. Even the mighty grizzly bear frequently roams through this rich habitat.

But be forewarned. There is one wildlife species you will see and not enjoy. This is the only section of trail in the park where we had to stop and get out the mosquito repellent and netting.

After enjoying the wildlife-rich area, retrace you steps to the trailhead.

**Side trips:** If you set up camp, you can hike up Berry Creek or do the Elk Ridge Loop hike before heading back to the trailhead.

# 14
# WILLOW FLATS LOOP

**General description:** A moderate day hike through a scenic flatland not far from civilization.

**Type of trip:** A "lollipop" loop.

**Total distance:** 8.3 miles.

**Starting point:** Jackson Lake Lodge.

**Traffic:** Heavy, including heavy horse use.

**Maps:** Earthwalk Press Grand Teton Map, NPS handout map, and a Colter Bay Trail Guide brochure published by the Grand Teton Natural History Association.

**Finding the trailhead:** Drive 15.2 miles south on U.S. 89 south of the park boundary, or 1 mile north of the Jackson Lake Junction with U.S. 287 and turn west into the well-marked Jackson Lake Lodge area. The trail actually starts in a small parking area on the south side of the main lodge.

**Parking and trailhead facilities:** Park in the Jackson Lake Lodge parking lot to use the restrooms or enjoy the restaurants and gift shops in the lodge.

**Key points:**
2.4 Junction with trail down Second Creek.
3.1 Concessionaire picnic area at Second Creek.
4.0 Junction with trail to Hermitage Point.
4.6 Junction with Willow Flats Trail.

# Willow Flats Loop

5.9  Junction with trail down Second Creek.
8.3  Jackson Lake Lodge.

**The hike:** This is a great hike for people staying at Jackson Lake Lodge, but pick a cool day because the route goes through open meadows and willow flats with very little shade along the way. Unlike trails in the high canyons of the Teton Range, snow leaves this area earlier in the spring and usually doesn't come as soon in the fall, which makes this route ideal for spring or fall hiking.

The route starts right behind Jackson Lake Lodge on a mostly abandoned jeep road, which is closed to the public but used occasionally by concessionaires serving meals to horse-riding groups. Actually, the entire route is on a dirt road, but it's still a pleasant hike, especially for hikers who get nervous about being too far from civilization and like perfectly flat hikes.

The first mile or so of the road goes through a large freshwater marsh. This is a wildlife-rich area, so you stand a good chance of seeing coyotes, moose, sandhill cranes, and other large wildlife species, as well as a wealth of smaller birds. You go by two classic beaver ponds and over Spring Creek on a bridge. You also get a great view of the Teton Range across Jackson Lake along the first part of the hike.

Cross the freshwater marsh and hike over Pilgrim Creek on a massive concrete bridge. Long ago, this was the main route into Jackson Hole. After U.S. 89 was constructed, this became a hiking trail with a monstrous, out-of-character bridge.

As you near the first junction, you enter a mixed forest area dominated by a stand of stately cottonwoods. When you reach the junction, take a left (south) onto another road leading to a concessionaire-operated picnic area for clients from Jackson Lake Lodge. You get a great view of the Teton Range with Second Creek in the foreground.

After the picnic area, you (finally!) get on a single-track trail through willow flats and grasslands. This trail is a little hard to find. It takes off to the right (west) about 100 yards before you reach the cooking area.

When you find the trail, turn right (west) and follow it through a very scenic and unusual flatland for 0.9 mile to the next junction, where you turn right (north) just before crossing Third Creek on a footbridge, again with a great view. From here, continue 0.6 mile along Third Creek until you reach the Willow Flats Road between Jackson Lake Lodge and Colter Bay. Turn right (east) here, and go 1.3 miles to the next junction, which marks the end of the loop section of the trail. Along this stretch conifers gradually give way to the stand of stately cottonwoods you hiked through earlier in the day.

From the junction, turn left (northeast) and retrace your steps back to Jackson Lake Lodge.

**Options:** This can be turned into a shorter (4.9-mile) shuttle between Jackson Lake Lodge and Colter Bay Corral. Refer to the Willow Flats Shuttle hike description. You can also take the loop section of this hike in reverse with no increase in difficulty.

# 15
# TWO OCEAN LAKE

**General description:** A medium-length hike around a large lake in a lesser known section of the park.
**Type of trip:** Loop, day hike.
**Total distance:** 6.4 miles.
**Difficulty:** Moderate.
**Starting point:** Two Ocean Picnic Area and Trailhead.
**Traffic:** Light.
**Maps:** Earthwalk Press Grand Teton Map and NPS handout map.

**Finding the trailhead:** From the Jackson Lake Junction, drive east on U.S. 287 for 2.6 miles and turn left (north) on the Pacific Creek Road. From the Moran Junction, drive west on U.S. 287 for 1.2 miles and turn right (north) onto the Pacific Creek Road. Drive 2 miles up the Pacific Creek Road before turning left (west) on the Two Ocean Road, which ends at the picnic area and trailhead 2.4 miles later. In the spring, heavy rains sometimes turn this road into a quagmire, and the NPS closes it, so be sure to check the status of the road at an entrance station or visitor center before making the trip up the Pacific Creek Road. The first part of the Pacific Creek Road is paved, but it turns into a good gravel road. The Two Ocean Road is also unpaved, and rougher than the Pacific Creek Road. It's 2.4 miles one way from

# Two Ocean Lake

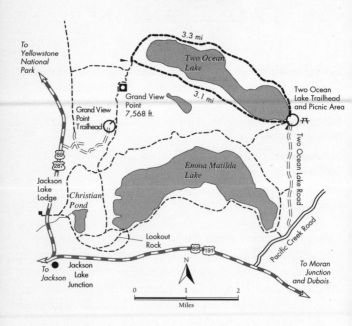

the Pacific Creek Road to the trailhead and picnic area. In good conditions, most vehicles can navigate both roads.

**Parking and trailhead facilities:** Park at the trailhead, which has picnic tables and a pit toilet.

## Key points:
3.3  Junction at the west end of lake.
6.4  Two Ocean Picnic Area.

**The hike:** When I took this hike in late June, I didn't see another hiker, which is next to amazing considering how nice this hike is. The reason? When you think of hiking in Grand Teton, you don't think of gentle trails around forest-lined mountain lakes. Instead, you think about walking around the great peaks. Consequently, it appears, the north-east corner of the park has been spared the popularity of the western section of the park.

You can take the loop from either direction. I liked the north shore better because it was more open, and the Teton Range was visible across the lake on the horizon. Since the morning is clear more often than the afternoon, you might try the north shore first.

Along the north shore, the trail splits several times. Take the high route, as the low route is for horses and has no footbridges over streams and marshy areas. Most of the north shore trail goes through meadows with consistently great scenery. The north shore route is also slightly longer than the south shore.

The south shore is more forested and has fewer views of the lake, but it has a few large meadows.

Watch for waterfowl on the lake and moose in the thickets lining both shores. Also, and most important, stay alert for signs of the great bear, as grizzlies are more common in this area than many parts of the park.

**Options:** You can take this loop in either direction with no extra difficulty. You can also start this loop at the Grand View Point Trailhead, a good option in the spring if the Two Ocean Road is closed.

**Side trips:** When you get to the west end of the lake, you can take a 2.6-mile trail (round trip) to the top of Grand View Point for a truly grand view of the lake you're hiking around. You can also take a 2-mile (round trip) trail from the picnic area to see Emma Matilda Lake.

# 16
# JENNY LAKE

**General description:** A great loop hike around the shoreline of one of the centerpieces of Grand Teton National Park.
**Type of trip:** Loop.
**Total distance:** 7.7 miles.
**Starting point:** String Lake Trailhead.
**Traffic:** Heavy.
**Maps:** Earthwalk Press Grand Teton Map and NPS handout map.

**Finding the trailhead:** Take U.S. 89 north of Jackson for 11.5 miles and turn left (west) at the Moose Junction. Drive past the Moose Visitor Center and through the entrance station (1 mile after turning off highway). Follow this paved park road for another 9.7 miles from the entrance station to the Jenny Lake turnoff. Turn left (west) here and drive 0.6 mile (follow the signs and take two right turns) to the String Lake Trailhead and Picnic Area. If you're coming from the north, drive 9.9 miles from the Jackson Lake Junction and turn right (west) at the Jenny Lake turnoff. If you plan to start at South Jenny Lake, go to the South Jenny Lake turnoff, which is 2.9 miles south of the Jenny Lake turnoff on the main park road.

**Parking and trailhead facilities:** Park in large parking lots at the trailhead or the picnic area. There are no toilet facilities right

# Jenny Lake

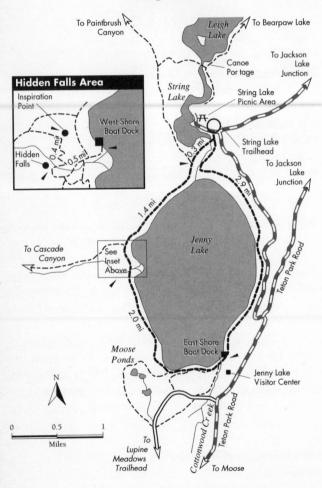

at the trailhead, but you can find them at the nearby picnic area. The South Jenny Lake area has a general store, visitor center, boat dock, toilet facilities, and plenty of room to park.

**Key points (from String Lake Trailhead):**

0.1  Bridge over outlet of String Lake.
0.5  Jenny Lake inlet.
2.2  West Shore boat dock and spur trail to Hidden Falls/ Inspiration Point.
4.0  Junction with Moose Ponds Trail.
4.3  Boat launching area.
4.5  Bridge over Cottonwood Creek, outlet of Jenny Lake.
4.6  East South Jenny Lake Boat Dock/Visitor Center, start of paved trail.
4.8  End of paved trail.
7.7  String Lake Trailhead.

**The hike:** There aren't many hikes of this distance that follow the shoreline of a beautiful lake the entire way. This makes the Jenny Lake Loop hike one of the most popular in Grand Teton National Park.

You can start at either South Jenny Lake or the String Lake Trailhead at the north end of Jenny Lake. This trail description follows the counterclockwise route starting from the String Lake Trailhead. This allows you to hike the more remote west side of the lake in the morning hours, stop for a snack at the South Jenny Lake general store, visit a visitor center without driving to it, and enjoy a scenic walk along the developed east shore after lunch.

The trail starts about 100 yards south of the trailhead parking lot at the bridge over the huge stream leaving String Lake. Go right (west) here and cross the bridge. In 0.2 mile, you turn left (south) at the junction with the String Lake Trail.

After this junction, hike along the unnamed stream between String Lake and Jenny Lake for about two-tenths of a mile to the first view of Jenny Lake at the inlet. From here, the trail follows the lakeshore until you get near the boat dock area on the west side of the lake. You won't see many hikers on the trail to the boat dock, but expect to see lots of people in the boat dock area, as the boat ride across Jenny Lake is very popular. Many park visitors take the boat to see Hidden Falls and Inspiration Point.

As you approach the boat dock area, the trail veers away from the lake slightly. You don't see the boat dock unless you take a short spur trail down to the lake. You might not need to do that, but you definitely want to take the 0.8 mile round trip up to see Hidden Falls and to soak in the view from Inspiration Point.

After being inspired from Inspiration Point, continue along the lake to the South Jenny Lake area. The trail closely follows the lakeshore after the boat dock area, but gradually pulls away from the lake as you reach the junction with the Moose Ponds trail. Go left (south) at this junction.

The west side trail gets rocky in a few places, but is mostly flat and uncrowded.

The developed southern section of Jenny Lake can get confusing, but stay on the trail near the lake, and you eventually come to the visitor center area. You pass by the Jenny

Lake boat launching area, a developed campground, other buildings and developments, and then over a long footbridge over the outlet of Jenny Lake (Cottonwood Creek), and on to the visitor center area. This is slightly more than halfway through the hike, so it's a good time to lay back, get a snack at the general store, and check out the interpretive displays in the visitor center before continuing up the east shore of the lake.

The trail through the developed area is paved, but the pavement ends about two-tenths of a mile up the lakeshore. The east shore is more heavily used than the west shore, and the one-way scenic drive parallels the trail for part of the way. However, the scenery could be considered better than the west shore. You get classic views of the high peaks across the lake and the trail is in better shape than on the west side.

**Options:** This loop hike can be taken in either direction with no extra difficulty. You can also make this a shuttle and skip the developed east side of the lake by leaving a vehicle at one end and hiking only the remote west side of the lake to see Hidden Falls. This cuts the total distance down to 4.6 miles.

**Side trips:** Don't miss the 0.4-mile (round trip) side trip to see Hidden Falls. Keep going up to Inspiration Point (another 0.4-mile round trip) for a panoramic view of Jenny Lake.

# Cascade Canyon

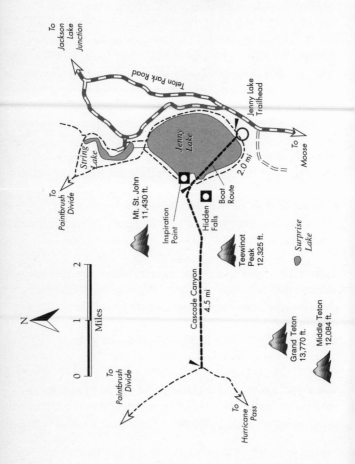

# 17
# CASCADE CANYON

**General description:** A classic hike into the main canyon below the Grand Teton.

**Type of trip:** Out and back.

**Total distance:** Up to 9.8 miles.

**Starting point:** Jenny Lake West Shore Boat Dock.

**Traffic:** Heavy.

**Maps:** Earthwalk Press Grand Teton Map and NPS handout map.

**Finding the trailhead:** Take U.S. 89 north of Jackson for 11.5 miles and turn left (west) at the Moose Junction. Drive past the Moose Visitor Center and through the entrance station (1 mile after turning off highway). Follow this paved park road for another 6.8 miles from the entrance station to the South Jenny Lake turnoff. Turn left (west) here and drive less than one-half mile to the South Jenny Lake boat dock and visitor center. If you're coming from the north, drive 12.8 miles from the Jackson Lake Junction and turn right (west) at the South Jenny Lake turnoff. From the South Jenny Lake boat dock, take the short boat ride across the lake to the west shore boat dock. The boat leaves every 15–20 minutes for a small fee.

**Parking and trailhead facilities:** The South Jenny Lake area has a general store, visitor center, boat dock, toilet facilities, and usually plenty of room to park. This is a heavily used area, and the boat ride across the lake is very popular, so in mid-day during the summer, the parking lot can be full. There are no facilities at the west shore boat dock.

### Key points:
0.2 Junction with Jenny Lake Trail.
0.5 Hidden Falls and junction with spur trail to Hidden Falls Overlook.
0.9 Inspiration Point.
1.6 Horse bypass trail.
4.9 Trail forks into South and North Fork Cascade Canyon Trails.

**The hike:** The mouth of Cascade Canyon around Hidden Falls is perhaps the most heavily used spot in Grand Teton National Park. Thousands of park visitors take the scenic boat ride across Jenny Lake and mill around the falls and Inspiration Point for awhile and then return. The area shows the wear and tear of this heavy use, but there's a reason for it: The falls are spectacular, and you definitely can get inspired by Inspiration Point.

Most visitors to Hidden Falls do not take the scenic hike up Cascade Canyon, so once you've gone past Inspiration Point, the traffic thins out dramatically.

The hike up the canyon climbs seriously for about the first mile and then goes into a gradual, almost unnoticeable ascent along the cascading stream. The steep canyon gives you one outstanding view after another all the way to the junction where the trail splits into the South Fork up to

Hurricane Pass and the North Fork to Lake Solitude and the Paintbrush Divide.

After a short rest, turn around here and retrace your steps back to Jenny Lake in time to catch the boat back across the lake. If for some reason you didn't catch the boat, you can hike along the south shore of the lake 2.1 miles to the east shore boat dock.

**Options:** If you want to leave early in the morning or don't like boats, you can hike along the south shore of Jenny Lake to get to the Hidden Falls area. This would add about 4 miles to your hike.

# 18
# SIGNAL MOUNTAIN

**General description:** The only trail in this section of the park with a unique view of Jackson Hole.
**Type of trip:** A "lollipop" loop.
**Total distance:** 7.4 miles.
**Starting point:** Signal Mountain Lodge.
**Traffic:** Light.
**Maps:** Earthwalk Press Grand Teton Map and NPS hand-out map.

**Finding the trailhead:** Take U.S. 89 north of Jackson for 11.5 miles and turn left (west) at the Moose Junction. Drive past the Moose Visitor Center and through the entrance station (1 mile after turning off the highway). Follow this paved park road for another 17 miles from the entrance station and turn left (west) into the Signal Mountain Lodge area. If you're coming from the north, drive 2.6 miles from the Jackson Lake Junction and turn right (west) at the Signal Mountain Lodge area.

This trailhead is quite difficult to find. Actually, it's at a small sign on the east side of the road about one-tenth of a mile south of the Signal Mountain Lodge turnoff. There is no place to pull off or park a car right at the trailhead, so it's easy to miss it. You can also start this hike from the boat launch area, but again, no parking spots.

# Signal Mountain

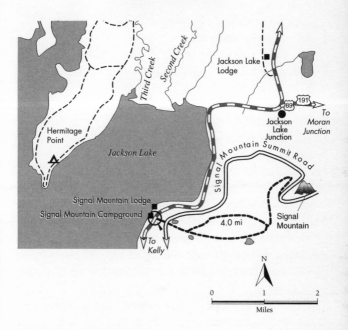

**Parking and trailhead facilities:** There is no place to park where the trail starts on the main park road, so park in the large parking lot in the lodge area. This adds about four-tenths of a mile to the total distance of this trip. There are restrooms, a general store, a restaurant, gift shops, a gas station, and a ranger station in the Signal Mountain area.

**Key points** (from Signal Mountain Lodge):
0.2  Trailhead on main park road.
0.4  Signal Mountain Summit Road.
0.7  Start of loop trail.
3.2  Spur trail to top of Signal Mountain.
3.7  Summit of Signal Mountain.
4.2  Loop trail.
6.7  End of loop.
7.0  Signal Mountain Road.
7.2  Trailhead on main park road.
7.4  Signal Mountain Lodge area.

**The hike:** This is the only official hike in this part of the park. From the top of Signal Mountain, you get a panoramic view of the entire valley—Jackson Lake and the Teton Range to the west and the Oxbow Bend of the Snake River to the north. Yes, you can drive to the top of Signal Mountain on a paved road, but you miss a great hike and some nice exercise if you do.

From the lodge area, carefully walk on and cross the highway to the trail. From here, you climb gradually to the junction with the loop trail, which is about three-tenths of a mile after crossing (again, carefully) paved Signal Mountain Road.

When you get to the start of the loop trail, you can take a left (northeast) on the "ridge route" or a right on the "lake route." It makes no difference, but this trail description takes the clockwise route. This loop does not show on commercial maps for the area, but it is on the NPS handout map.

The ridge route goes through mature forest and large

sagebrush meadows. When you get halfway around the loop, you see the spur trail going off to the top of the mountain. This is a must-see side trip and adds about 1 mile to the total distance of the trip. The view from the top is so much more rewarding when you walk up there.

After you rejoin the loop trail, go left (south) and continue through a big meadow until you drop down to the more forested area around Keith Lake (watch for many species of waterfowl on the lake) and then back to the start of the loop. Go left (west) here, and retrace your steps back to the lodge area. The trail is in great shape and easy to follow the entire way.

Commercial maps and the NPS handout show a trail going from the top of the ridge north to Oxbow Bend, but this trail has been abandoned because of the unsafe condition of the old bridge over the Snake River.

**Options:** If you don't like hills, you can, of course, get a ride to the top and walk down to the lodge.

# Hermitage Point

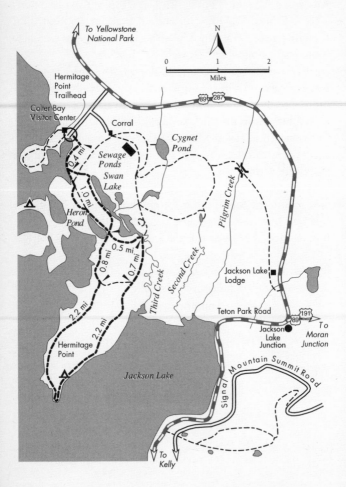

# 19
# HERMITAGE POINT

**General description:** A unique hike on an undeveloped penin-
sula in expansive Jackson Lake.
**Type of trip:** A "lollipop" loop.
**Total distance:** 9.4 miles.
**Starting point:** Hermitage Point Trailhead.
**Traffic:** Heavy to moderate.
**Maps:** Earthwalk Press Grand Teton Map, NPS handout
map, and a Colter Bay Trail Guide brochure published by
the Grand Teton Natural History Association.

**Finding the trailhead:** Take U.S. 89 into the park and turn west
into the Colter Bay area, which is 11 miles south of the
park's northern boundary or 5.2 miles north of the Jackson
Lake Junction with U.S. 287. The trailhead is a little hard
to find the first time you go into the Colter Bay area. It's
located at the southern end of the big parking lot near the
boat launch. After turning into Colter Bay from the main
highway, drive 0.9 mile on a paved road to the trailhead,
turning left (south) at the first turn after passing the general
store. Be careful not to take the trail heading off to the east
behind the trailhead sign. Instead, walk to the end of the
parking lot toward the boat launch where you see the
trailhead signs marking the beginning of the trail.

**Parking and trailhead facilities:** Park in the large parking lot at the trailhead. The lot is also used for people launching boats. Go to the visitor center (just north of trailhead) for restrooms. You pass a general store on the way to the trailhead.

**Key points:**
0.4 Junction with Swan Lake Trail.
0.6 Junction with Jackson Lake Overlook Trail, alternate route.
1.0 Heron Pond.
1.4 Four-way junction.
2.2 Junction with cutoff trail.
4.4 Hermitage Point.
4.9 Designated campsite No. 9.
6.6 Junction with cutoff trail.
7.3 Junction with trail to Heron Pond.
7.8 Heron Pond and four-way junction.
8.3 Swan Lake.
8.9 Junction with trail to Colter Bay Corral.
9.0 Rejoin main trail to Colter Bay area.
9.4 Hermitage Point Trailhead.

**The hike:** The Hermitage Point area is a confusing labyrinth of trails. After hiking all of them, I recommend this route as among the best hikes in the park. This is essentially an extended version of the Swan Lake and Heron Pond hike (Hike 4).

Be sure to take a map and plan on closely noting the directional signs along the route. There are several junctions along this short loop, and if you're enjoying the scenery too thoroughly (which would be easy), you might get on the wrong trail.

The trail starts out as a service road (it has a locked gate and is only occasionally used by vehicles). Along this stretch of trail, you can enjoy outstanding views of Colter Bay with Mount Moran providing a classic backdrop.

At the end of the dirt road, you reach the first junction where the loop section of this trip begins. Go right (south), unless you decide to take the route in reverse. The trail goes back to singletrack, but it's still in excellent shape.

About two-tenths of a mile later, you reach a fork in the trail. If you don't mind a little hill, go right for a nice view from the Jackson Lake Overlook. Either trail takes you to Heron Pond about one-half mile later.

Heron Pond is mostly covered with pond lilies. You can usually see pelicans, Canada geese, and other waterfowl species on the pond. In the evening hours, you might see beavers dining on the pond lilies, or you might see a moose in the willows that surround the pond.

At the south end of Heron Pond, you reach a four-way trail junction. Take the extreme right turn, and keep heading south along the lakeshore. You return to this junction later in the hike. In 0.8 mile, turn right (south) again at the junction with the cutoff trail.

After leaving Heron Pond, the trail stays out of sight of Jackson Lake for awhile, and then enters an open sagebrush flat with totally stunning views of the Teton Range, especially Mount Moran, across Hermitage Point. It stays this way for about 1 mile to the point.

After a rest to enjoy the scenery at the point, continue through the sagebrush meadows as you head back along the east side of the peninsula, past campsite No. 9, to the junction with the cutoff trail. Go right (north) at this junction, and hike another 0.7 mile to the second cutoff trail. Here, take a left (west) and go over a small hill and down to the four-way junction at the south end of Heron Pond. At this junction, take the first right (not the trail along the shore of Heron Pond) and go north back over the small ridge down to Swan Lake.

Like Heron Pond, Swan Lake is covered with yellow pond lilies. The lake gets its name from the same two trumpeter swans that have lived here since the 1980s. The rare swans have never produced any young, but they have fiercely defended their territory, chasing away other swans that might have successfully nested in this prime habitat.

After the lake, you pass by abandoned sewage ponds and then to a junction with a trail heading off to the right (north) to the Colter Bay Corral. Go left (west) and 0.1 mile later, rejoin the abandoned service road for a 0.4 mile walk back to the trailhead.

**Options:** This route has many options—so many, in fact, that it can get confusing. You can take the cutoff trail to knock 4.4 miles off the trip, but you miss outstanding scenery from Hermitage Point. You can also go north at the second cutoff trail, but you miss Swan Lake.

# 20
# SURPRISE AND
# AMPHITHEATER LAKES

**General description:** A popular hike to two high-country lakes in the shadow of the Grand Teton.
**Type of trip:** Out-and-back.
**Total distance:** 9.6 miles.
**Starting point:** Lupine Meadows Trailhead.
**Traffic:** Heavy.
**Maps:** Earthwalk Press Grand Teton Map and NPS handout map.

**Finding the trailhead:** Take U.S. 89 north of Jackson for 11.5 miles and turn left (west) at the Moose Junction. Drive past the Moose Visitor Center and through the entrance station (1 mile after turning off highway). Follow this paved park road for another 6.6 miles from the entrance station and turn left (west) onto a gravel road at the Lupine Meadows turnoff. Follow this road for 1.4 miles until it ends at the trailhead parking lot. If you're coming from the north, drive 21.8 miles from the Jackson Lake Junction and turn right (west) at the Lupine Meadows turnoff.

**Parking and trailhead facilities:** The trailhead has toilet facilities and a huge parking area, but this trailhead is so popular that it can be full, especially at midday. You can find a general store at the South Jenny Lake turnoff about a mile to the north.

# Surprise and Amphitheater Lakes

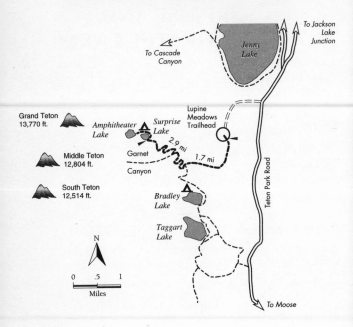

## Key points:
1.7 Junction with trail to Bradley Lake.
3.0 Junction with trail to Garnet Canyon.
4.6 Surprise Lake.
4.8 Amphitheater Lake.

**The hike:** This is one of the most popular hikes in the park, so expect to see lots of people on the trail and a large parking lot full of vehicles at the trailhead.

From Lupine Meadows, the first 0.5 mile of the trail goes through mature forest with nice views of Grand Teton off to the right and then climbs up a ridge to the junction with the Garnet Canyon Trail, which also goes to Surprise and Amphitheater Lakes. Turn right (west) here and start a series of switchbacks up to the lakes. At several points, you get sweeping views of Bradley and Taggart Lakes to the southeast and Jenny Lake to the northeast, as well as the rest of the valley floor.

At the 3-mile mark, turn right (west) again at the junction with the trail up Garnet Canyon.

When you get to Surprise Lake, the only surprise will be how beautiful it is, with Teepee Pillar, Disappointment Peak, Mount Owen, and much more of the Teton Range, including the Grand Teton, majestically looming in the background over the lake. Amphitheater Lake, only 0.2 mile up the trail, is at least as nice, with an amphitheater view of the high peaks.

After enjoying the two gems of the Teton Range, retrace your steps to the Lupine Meadows Trailhead.

**Side trips:** You can take the side trip up to the end of Garnet Canyon, which adds 2.2 miles to the total distance of your trip.

# Preserving Grand Teton

The Grand Teton Natural History Association is a non-profit organization founded to assist with educational, historical, and scientific programs in and around Grand Teton National Park. The Association operates bookstores in the park and in the nearby National Elk Refuge and Bridger-Teton National Forest. When you buy a book, video, or map from one of these bookstores, the profit goes to benefit educational and interpretation programs in the park. Your purchase also supports the publication of educational brochures available at information counters and entrance stations.

You can obtain a mail-order catalog of products offered by the Association by writing Grand Teton Natural History Association, P.O. Box 170, Moose, Wyoming 83012. You can also visit the Association's website at www.grandteton.com/gnha for more information.

## About the Author

Bill Schneider has spent more than 30 years hiking trails all across America and has written nine other hiking guides.

During college in the mid-1960s, he worked on a trail crew in Glacier National Park. He then spent the 1970s publishing *Montana Outdoors* magazine for the Montana Department of Fish, Wildlife, and Parks and covering as many miles of trail as possible on weekends and holidays.

In 1979, Bill and his partner, Mike Sample, created Falcon Press Publishing Company and released two guidebooks that first year. Bill wrote one of them, *Hiking Montana*, which is still popular. Since then, he has written 17 other books and many magazine articles on wildlife, outdoor recreation, and environmental issues. Along the way, on a part-time basis over a span of 12 years, Bill has taught classes on bicycling, backpacking, no-trace camping, and hiking in bear country for the Yellowstone Institute, a nonprofit educational organization in Yellowstone National Park.

Today, Bill still serves as president and publisher of Falcon Publishing, which is now the leading national publisher of recreational guidebooks, with more than 700 titles in print, most of them published as part of the popular FalconGuide series.

get
**FALCON** GUIDED

**FALCON** GUIDES are available for where-to-go hiking, mountain biking, rock climbing, walking, scenic driving, fishing, rockhounding, paddling, birding, wildlife viewing, and camping. We also have FalconGuides on essential outdoor skills and subjects and field identification. The following titles are currently available, but this list grows every year. For a free catalog with a complete list of titles, call FALCON toll-free at 1-800-582-2665.

■ *To order any of these books, check with your local bookseller*
*or call FALCON® at* **1-800-582-2665**.
*Visit us on the world wide web at:*
www.falconguide.com

FALCON®

## SCENIC DRIVING GUIDES

Scenic Driving Alaska and the Yukon
Scenic Driving Arizona
Scenic Driving the Beartooth Highway
Scenic Driving California
Scenic Driving Colorado
Scenic Driving Florida
Scenic Driving Georgia
Scenic Driving Hawaii
Scenic Driving Idaho
Scenic Driving Michigan
Scenic Driving Minnesota
Scenic Driving Montana
Scenic Driving New England
Scenic Driving New Mexico
Scenic Driving North Carolina
Scenic Driving Oregon
Scenic Driving the Ozarks
Scenic Driving Pennsylvania
Scenic Driving Texas
Scenic Driving Utah
Scenic Driving Washington
Scenic Driving Wisconsin
Scenic Driving Wyoming
Scenic Driving Yellowstone and Grand
   Teton National Parks
Scenic Byways East
Scenic Byways Far West
Scenic Byways Rocky Mountains
Back Country Byways
Traveling California's Gold Rush Country
Traveling the Lewis & Clark Trail
Traveling the Oregon Trail
Traveler's Guide to the Pony Express Trail

## WILDLIFE VIEWING GUIDES

Alaska Wildlife Viewing Guide
Arizona Wildlife Viewing Guide
California Wildlife Viewing Guide
Colorado Wildlife Viewing Guide
Florida Wildlife Viewing Guide
Indiana Wildlife Vewing Guide
Iowa Wildlife Viewing Guide
Kentucky Wildlife Viewing Guide
Massachusetts Wildlife Viewing Guide
Montana Wildlife Viewing Guide
Nebraska Wildlife Viewing Guide
Nevada Wildlife Viewing Guide
New Hampshire Wildlife Viewing Guide
New Jersey Wildlife Viewing Guide
New Mexico Wildlife Viewing Guide
New York Wildlife Viewing Guide
North Carolina Wildlife Viewing Guide
North Dakota Wildlife Viewing Guide
Ohio Wildlife Viewing Guide
Oregon Wildlife Viewing Guide
Puerto Rico & the Virgin Islands
   Wildlife Viewing Guide
Tennessee Wildlife Viewing Guide
Texas Wildlife Viewing Guide
Utah Wildlife Viewing Guide
Vermont Wildlife Viewing Guide
Virginia Wildlife Viewing Guide
Washington Wildlife Viewing Guide
West Virginia Wildife Viewing Guide
Wisconsin Wildlife Viewing Guide

# FALCON GUIDES® Leading the Way™

**All books in this popular series are regularly updated with accurate information on access, side trips, & safety.**

## HIKING GUIDES

Best Hikes Along the Continental Divide
Hiking Alaska
Hiking Arizona
Hiking Arizona's Cactus Country
Hiking the Beartooths
Hiking Big Bend National Park
Hiking the Bob Marshall Country
Hiking California
Hiking California's Desert Parks
Hiking Carlsbad Caverns & Guadalupe Mtns.
    National Parks
Hiking Colorado
Hiking Colorado, Vol. II
Hiking Colorado's Summits
Hiking Colorado's Weminuche Wilderness
Hiking the Columbia River Gorge
Hiking Florida
Hiking Georgia
Hiking Glacier/Waterton Lakes
Hiking Grand Canyon National Park
Hiking Grand Staircase-Escalante
Hiking Grand Teton National Park
Hiking Great Basin
Hiking Hot Springs in the Pacific NW
Hiking Idaho
Hiking Maine
Hiking Michigan
Hiking Minnesota
Hiking Montana
Hiking Mount Rainier National Park
Hiking Mount St. Helens
Hiking Nevada
Hiking New Hampshire
Hiking New Mexico
Hiking New York
Hiking North Carolina
Hiking North Cascades
Hiking Northern Arizona
Hiking Olympic National Park
Hiking Oregon

Hiking Oregon's Eagle Cap Wilderness
Hiking Oregon's Mt Hood/Badger Creek
Hiking Oregon's Three Sisters Country
Hiking Pennsylvania
Hiking Shenandoah National Park
Hiking the Sierra Nevada
Hiking South Carolina
Hiking South Dakota's Black Hills Cntry
Hiking Southern New England
Hiking Tennessee
Hiking Texas
Hiking Utah
Hiking Utah's Summits
Hiking Vermont
Hiking Virginia
Hiking Washington
Hiking Wyoming
Hiking Wyoming's Cloud Peak Wilderness
Hiking Wyoming's Wind River Range
Hiking Yellowstone National Park
Hiking Zion & Bryce Canyon
Exploring Canyonlands & Arches
Exploring Hawaii's Parklands

## BEST EASY DAY HIKES

Beartooths
Canyonlands & Arches
Cape Cod
Colorado Springs
Glacier & Waterton Lakes
Grand Canyon
Grand Staircase-Escalante/Glen Cny
Grand Teton
Lake Tahoe
Mount Rainier
Mount St. Helens
North Cascades
Olympics
Salt Lake City
Shenandoah
Yellowstone

FALCON®

# MORE THAN 5 MILLION COPIES SOLD!

# FALCON GUIDES® Leading the Way™

## PADDLING GUIDES

Floater's Guide to Colorado
Paddling Montana
Paddling Okefenokee
Paddling Oregon
Paddling Yellowstone/Grand Teton

## ROCK CLIMBING GUIDES

Rock Climbing Colorado
Rock Climbing Montana
Rock Climbing New Mexico & Texas
Rock Climbing Utah
Rock Climbing Washington

## ROCKHOUNDING GUIDES

Rockhounding Arizona
Rockhounding California
Rockhounding Colorado
Rockhounding Montana
Rockhounding Nevada
Rockhound's Guide to New Mexico
Rockhounding Texas
Rockhounding Utah
Rockhounding Wyoming

## BIRDING GUIDES

Birding Minnesota
Birding Montana
Birding Northern California
Birding Texas
Birding Utah

## FIELD GUIDES

Bitterroot: Montana State Flower
Canyon Country Wildflowers
Central Rocky Mountains Wildflowers
Great Lakes Berry Book
New England Berry Book
Pacific Northwest Berry Book
Plants of Arizona
Rare Plants of Colorado
Rocky Mountain Berry Book
Scats & Tracks of the Pacific Coast States
Scats & Tracks of the Rocky Mountains
Tallgrass Prairie Wildflowers
Western Trees
Wildflowers of Southwestern Utah
Willow Bark and Rosehips

## WALKING

Walking Colorado Springs
Walking Denver
Walking Portland
Walking St. Louis
Walking Virginia Beach

## FISHING GUIDES

Fishing Alaska
Fishing the Beartooths
Fishing Florida
Fishing Glacier National Park
Fishing Maine
Fishing Montana
Fishing Wyoming
Fishing Yellowstone

To order check with you local bookseller or
call FALCON® at **1-800-582-2665**.
www.FalconOutdoors.com

FALCON®